Beetles

by Alice Mead

illustrated by Virge Kask

MODERN CURRICULUM PRESS

Pearson Learning Group

Are all ladybugs ladies? Why do fireflies glow in the dark? Do tumble bugs really tumble? Maybe you have asked yourself these questions before. But did you know that all these insects are beetles?

Stag-Horned Beetles

There are over 300,000 kinds of beetles! In fact, beetles are the most common animal in the world.

Beetles are part of a large group of insects called *arthropods* (ARTH-roh-pods), meaning "jointed legs." But the beetle is the only kind of arthropod that has both hard and soft wings. The hard wings create a shell that protects the beetle from attack.

Beetles come in many different shapes, sizes, and colors. The smallest beetle is only one-fiftieth of an inch long. One of the biggest beetles, called the Goliath beetle, is about five inches long!

A beetle's body is made up of three main parts: the head, the thorax, and the abdomen. Did you know that your body also has these three parts? Try comparing yourself to a beetle. If you were a beetle, you would have no bones. In place of skin, you would have a hard shell made of material much like your fingernails. You would have six legs to move. You might have curved, sharp jaws to make holes in trees.

You would sense life in a different way than you do now. You might taste with feelers instead of a tongue. Each of your eyes has one lens. But a beetle's eye can have many lenses. Some have 2,500 lenses in one eye!

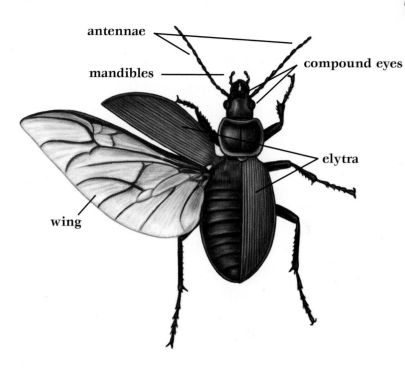

antennae

mandibles

compound eyes

elytra

wing

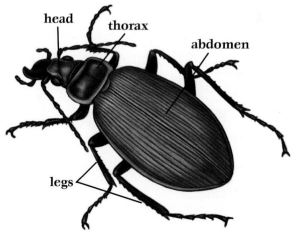

head

thorax

abdomen

legs

5

People have been interested in beetles for thousands of years. Five thousand years ago, people in ancient Egypt were very curious about the beetles they saw. They were known as scarab beetles. The scarab was very important to the ancient Egyptians. They made beautiful jewelry of gold and precious stones in the shape of the scarab beetles. They used these as charms.

Egyptians noticed that first, the adult scarab beetle gathered together a ball of dung from the goats and camels in the courtyards. Then the beetle pushed this smooth ball, or pellet, down a hole.

Down inside the hole, the female beetle laid her eggs in these pellets. That way, when the eggs hatched, the dung provided food for them.

In America, children call scarab beetles "tumble bugs."

adult

eggs

larva

pupa

8

Like many other insects, beetles grow in four steps.

First, the female beetle lays eggs, usually hundreds of them. She lays them in a protected place near food so her young can eat after they hatch.

After about four weeks, each egg hatches. Out crawls a soft, pale worm. This is called a *larva* (LAHR-vah). Although the larva looks soft, it has strong jaws. A larva is an eating machine. As it eats, it grows and grows.

When the larva is finished growing, it finds a quiet spot beneath some leaves or underground. It grows a hard case called a *pupa* (PYOO-pah). Inside the case, the adult beetle is now forming.

Finally, the beetle grows legs and wings. In two or three weeks, the adult beetle climbs out of the pupa case. The outer wing has hardened. If the beetle is a flyer, then the soft wing is ready for flight.

Fireflies are one of the most interesting kinds of beetle. There are almost two thousand different kinds of this beetle, all over the world.

Fireflies are a very primitive form of beetle. They developed millions and millions of years ago—even before dinosaurs!

Scientists think fireflies formed when there was little oxygen in the Earth's atmosphere. They believe that the glowing light in the firefly's abdomen is left over from that early time.

You could compare the firefly and its ability to make light to primitive fish who live deep in the sea in total darkness. They too have the ability to make light. It is called *bioluminescence* (bi-oh-lu-min-ESS-ens).

Today, fireflies use their flickers as signals. The lights help the male firefly in the air and the female firefly hidden in the grass find one another. They flicker light back and forth.

In June, the female firefly lays about two hundred eggs in the grass. June is a good time to hunt for fireflies.

If you do catch a firefly, be gentle. Place it in a jar with holes in the lid for air. Observe your firefly from up close. Then let it go. You can observe other beetles in the same way.

Fireflies are not born looking or acting like fireflies at all. Instead, like all beetles, the firefly grows in four stages.

Out of the egg, a soft, worm-like larva hatches. The larva glimmers softly with bioluminescence. It is called a glowworm. Without a hard shell, life is dangerous for the small glowworm. It can be eaten by other beetles or even crushed by a heavy rain.

The job of the larva is to eat and eat. During the day, it hides under a stone. At night, it comes out looking in damp places for slugs, snails, and cutworms. The glowworm is able to eat such big creatures because of a special chemical. When it bites a snail, the chemical softens and paralyzes the snail. Then the little glowworm can eat it. Other beetles use this method too.

Larva

Pupa

The glowworm helps gardeners. Snails, slugs, and cutworms can destroy crops overnight!

The firefly larva eats and grows for one to two years. During the winter, the glowworm, like many other beetles and larva, hides under a stone. The larva stays still and dormant like a frog or turtle until warm air returns.

In the spring, it hardens into a pupa shell. In a few weeks, the adult firefly emerges from the pupa.

After all this growing and eating, the adult firefly never eats at all!

It lives for only three weeks. During that time, using its flickering tail signals, it must find a mate, lay eggs, and die.

The life cycle starts again with the hatching of the new eggs.

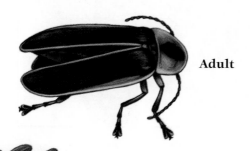

Adult

Ladybugs are also beetles. In fact, they used to be called ladybird beetles. (No, they are not all females!) Scientists have studied thousands of kinds of these beetles.

Gardeners have always liked ladybugs. They are useful beetles because they eat harmful insects like *aphids* (AY-fids).

But now, in some states, there are too many of these little orange and black-dotted ladybird beetles. The balance of nature has been disrupted.

It is October. In Vermont and other northern states, the leaves of the maple trees are bright red and orange. But now there is another bright splash of color as well.

A new type of ladybug has come to the northern United States. The North American ladybug spends the winter months in the base of trees. It makes little burrows for warmth until spring.

But the new ladybugs like to hide for the winter in narrow, dark cracks of walls. And where do they find those walls? On warm, sunny October days, ladybugs fly to the outside walls of people's houses. They especially like white houses.

When the colorful little beetles land on a house, they look for a crack, often around a window frame. Then they crawl inside. One family estimated that they had thirty thousand ladybugs in their house!

These ladybugs were probably brought to our country by ships from Asia. If you find them in your house, don't worry. They won't do any harm.

Beetles account for nearly half of all the world's insect population. They live on the ground, under the ground, in the air, and even in water.

In the air, the adult beetle is a clumsy flyer. It has a heavy, armored body. The beetle uses only one set of its wings to fly. The hard wings open up so that the soft wings flap. A beetle flies in an up-and-down pattern, as though it were riding over waves.

Most beetles are scavengers. They search for dead material with their feelers.

The beetle finds a dead woodland animal, such as a mole. It inspects the mole's body to see how big it is.

Then it digs dirt from underneath the mole and lowers the body into the dirt.

Sexton Beetle

Carrion Beetle

Next the beetle digs a tunnel. It climbs into the tunnel and lays eggs. The larva will feed on the body of the dead mole.

Some beetles bore holes through wood to lay eggs. These beetles can cause great damage to trees. After the eggs hatch, each larva eats tunnels through the wood. Most beetles live only a few weeks to one year as larva.

Ground Beetle

Some beetles live in ponds and streams. Diving beetles, whirligigs, and crawling water beetles are some of these insects. Water beetles are similar to land beetles, but their back legs are flat and covered with hairs. The beetles' back legs are like paddles. They help the insects move easily through the water.

Whirligig

Great Diving Beetle

Crawling Water Beetle

Water beetles have breathing holes along the sides of their bodies. Some of them trap air under their back wings before a deep dive. That way they have a pocket of oxygen next to their breathing holes.

Diving beetles are predators. They eat insects, snails, and even small fish—or tadpoles! Like all beetles, they spend their lives finding food and hiding from predators.

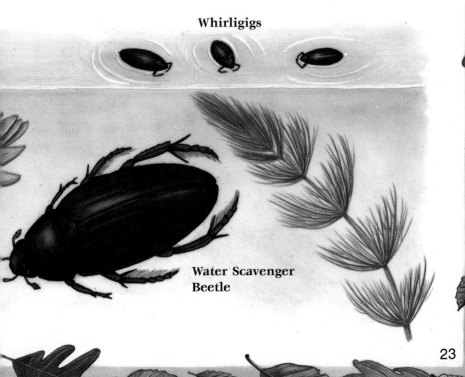

Whirligigs

Water Scavenger Beetle

Entomologists (people who study insects) have identified 300,000 kinds of beetles. How? By careful observation!

You can learn more about beetles by observing them too. Visit a nature center, or ask a science teacher in your school to show you some preserved insects.

Or, better yet, walk around your neighborhood or a local park. Keep your eyes open for different insects. See if you can identify which insects are beetles. With 300,000 different kinds of beetles, you're sure to bump into a few.